Biarritz
Travel Guide

Quick Trips Series

No part of this publication may be reproduced, stored in a retrieval system, or transmitted, in any form or by any means without the prior written permission of the publisher, nor be otherwise circulated in any form of binding or cover other than that in which it is published and without similar condition being imposed on the subsequent purchaser. If there are any errors or omissions in copyright acknowledgements the publisher will be pleased to insert the appropriate acknowledgement in any subsequent printing of this publication. Although we have taken all reasonable care in researching this book we make no warranty about the accuracy or completeness of its content and disclaim all liability arising from its use.

Copyright © 2016, Astute Press
All Rights Reserved.

Table of Contents

BIARRITZ & THE FRENCH BASQUE COUNTRY　6
- Customs & Culture 8
- Geography 10
- Weather & Best Time to Visit 13

SIGHTS & ACTIVITIES: WHAT TO SEE & DO　14
- Biarritz 14
  - History Museum 15
  - Virgin on the Rock 16
  - Museum of the Sea 17
  - City of the Ocean 18
  - Asiatic and Oriental Art Museum 19
  - Biarritz Lighthouse 20
- Bayonne 21
  - Cazenave Chocolate Shop & Tea Room 23
  - Saint Mary's Cathedral & Cloister 24
  - History Museum of the Basques 25
  - Bonnat Museum 26
- Saint Jean-de-Luz 28
  - Saint John the Baptist Church 29
  - House of Louis XIV 30
- St.-Jean-Pied-de-Port 31

    Cheese Cave...33
    Bishop's Prison..33
☯ ROUTE DE CORNICHE (BETWEEN SAINT-JEAN-DE-LUZ & HENDAYE) 35
☯ LITTLE TRAIN OF LA RHUNE 36
☯ VILLA ARNAGA HOUSE & GARDENS 38
☯ GROTTOS OF ISTURITZ & OXOCELHAYA 40
☯ BASQUE CAKE MUSEUM 42
☯ CHATEAU ABBADIA 43
☯ LA-PIERRE-ST-MARTIN SKI RESORT 45
☯ ETXOLA ANIMAL PARK 47

BUDGET TIPS   49

☯ ACCOMMODATION 49
    Maison E. Bernat 49
    Quick Palace Anglet 51
    Manoir Théas 51
    Hotel Club Vacanciel Salies de Bearn 53
    Hotel Uhainak 54

☯ RESTAURANTS, CAFÉS & BARS 55
    Chez Mattin 55
    Auberge Du Petit Bayonne 56
    Bar Jean 57
    Restaurant les Trois Fontaines 58
    Ttotta 59

☯ SHOPPING 60

Bayonne Markets 60
Saint-Jean-de-Luz 62
Pau-Pyrenees 62
Accoceberry 63
Ainciart-Bergara 64

KNOW BEFORE YOU GO — 66

- ENTRY REQUIREMENTS 66
- HEALTH INSURANCE 67
- TRAVELLING WITH PETS 67
- AIRPORTS 68
- AIRLINES 70
- CURRENCY 71
- BANKING & ATMS 71
- CREDIT CARDS 71
- TOURIST TAXES 72
- RECLAIMING VAT 72
- TIPPING POLICY 73
- MOBILE PHONES 73
- DIALLING CODE 74
- EMERGENCY NUMBERS 74
- TIME ZONE 75
- DAYLIGHT SAVINGS TIME 76
- SCHOOL HOLIDAYS 76
- DRIVING LAWS 76
- DRINKING LAWS 77
- SMOKING LAWS 78
- ELECTRICITY 78

Food & Drink 79

BIARRITZ TRAVEL GUIDE

Biarritz & the French Basque Country

The "real" South of France is not just the French Riviera on the Mediterranean. On the western side of the country is the French Basque region with the Atlantic crashing onto its shores. Here you will find beautiful resort towns including Biarritz – a favourite of Sir Winston Churchill and many other famous foreigners.

BIARRITZ TRAVEL GUIDE

The history of the Basque country can be traced back to Roman times and the region served for many centuries as a crossroads for major armies passing through on their way to Portugal and Spain. The region itself has been the subject of many conflicts and control has changed hands often and suffered as a consequence.

The culture of the French Basque people is more linked to Spain than France, there is a shared coastline and the Pyrénées form a mountainous boundary between large parts of the two countries.

The Basques are one of the oldest cultures in Europe and as the land is relatively mountainous they remain fairly isolated from the rest of their countries. On the French side about a quarter of the population speak Basque, rather than the official language of French.

BIARRITZ TRAVEL GUIDE

This unusual and often difficult to understand language is a traditional part of Basque heritage and is one of a kind. There have been many theories as to the origins of the Basque people; refugees from Atlantis and the lost tribes from Israel being two of the more popular ones.

If you drive through the countryside of the French Basque country you will sometimes forget you are actually in France. Not only is the architecture different but the surrounding countryside is decidedly non-French. In Bayonne the houses stand tall and narrow, squeezed together like soldiers from different regiments mixed up so their uniforms clash.

This Extea style of architecture dates from the 17th and 18th centuries. The rolling green hills contain tiny villages

BIARRITZ TRAVEL GUIDE

like Ainhoa, which is one of the most beautiful villages in France and a lovely place to stop if you are driving along the Route de Saint-Jacques. This tiny village is approximately 20 kilometres south of Bayonne and right on the French-Spanish border. There is a border crossing a few kilometres south of Ainhoa at Dantxana if you want to visit Spain.

🌎 Customs & Culture

After the French Revolution the French Basque people lost much of their autonomy but their culture and traditions are still apparent all over the region. Many of the inhabitants still wear the traditional dress of berets and espadrilles. The espadrille was made famous by Gaston Lagaffe and is an essential part of the summer wardrobe in this region. Traditional products to find are Basque

BIARRITZ TRAVEL GUIDE

linen which is fabric with colourful stripes and a mahkila, a unique walking stick with a concealed spike

The French Basque region is full of brightly coloured local life and traditions. Most weekends there will be music and dancing in the plazas of the towns and villages. The Basque people are friendly with a ready smile, so even if you can't understand a word they say, smile back! While being a world away from Paris and fiercely independent the Basques are quite happy to sip a café au lait and to play boules while watching the tricolour or Ikurriña flag flying. A popular drink in the French Basque Country is Izarra, a herb liqueur available in yellow or green and around 40° proof.

The local Espelette spicy pepper is used in many Basque dishes. The pepper even has its own festival when in

BIARRITZ TRAVEL GUIDE

October every year the town of Espelette holds a two-day celebration for this little red devil. The streets and houses are festooned with thousands of red peppers hanging out to dry and on the Sunday morning everyone attends church to give thanks for the harvest. With crowds of around 20,000 every year there is plenty of food about, mostly flavoured with pepper of course.

In the summer months most villages hold a fête that lasts all weekend. Eating, drinking and dancing on the Saturday continues into the small hours (join in and be glad you won't have to get up at an ungodly hour to milk the cows!) Sunday brings competitions to demonstrate just how much testosterone there is in the village with competitions of strength and stamina. Individuals and teams take part and some events involve the men wearing a corset type garment to prevent hernias.

BIARRITZ TRAVEL GUIDE

🌐 Geography

The French Basque Country is in the southwest of the country and the region shares the Pyrénéan Mountains with Spain. The region extends from the Pyrénées and Anie Peak at 2,503 metres (8,213 feet) to the rugged coasts of Biarritz and the flat beaches of Saint-Jean-de-Luz. Modern day French Basque country is divided into three provinces; Labourd, Lower Navarre and Soule although some people would argue there are five, and the areas of Bayonne and Gramont should be classed as provinces.

The French Basque country accounts for less than 12 per cent of the land surface of France, covering just less than 3,000 sq. km, and around nine per cent of the population. It is one of the poorer regions of France with the coastal areas being slightly better off due to tourism.

BIARRITZ TRAVEL GUIDE

In this part of France there around 30,000 companies, 66% in the service sector, 14% in the manufacturing sector and the remaining 20% covers a mixture of agriculture, farming, fishing and forestry. The French Basque country still relies heavily on sheep farming and in parts you will see white, fleecy sheep dotted across the landscape. The other main industries in the region are metalwork, food processing and aeronautics. Dassault Aviation is one of the biggest employers in the Basque country.

The French Basque country is easily accessible by train and Bayonne railway station is on the main line between Lisbon, Paris and Madrid. If you want to stay closer to the ground the road network is good from whichever direction you approach the region and the local bus services are efficient and cheap. For flying into the region there are quite a few choices. Biarritz Airport is six kilometres outside the town and is called Aéroport Biarritz-Anglet-Bayonne and is close to these towns as well. The unofficial name is Aéroport de Parme. Lourdes Airport is close by for the more northern part of the region and San Sebastián Airport in Spain is only 35 kilometres to the south of Biarritz. Pamplona Airport is just over the Spanish / French border as well.

The French Basque Region Map is here:

http://goo.gl/maps/Rzq7G

🌍 Weather & Best Time to Visit

Spring in the French Basque country can be wet, but the sun stays out for about six hours a day when it does come out of hiding and the average high goes from 14ºC in March to 18ºC in April. It can be cool at night so take a

BIARRITZ TRAVEL GUIDE

jumper if you are going to venture out after dark. In the summer heavy showers are common but soon clear away leaving bright blue skies and sunshine.

The afternoon temperatures in summer are between 22-26° C with night times staying pleasantly warm. Autumn brings a sharp drop with the temperature dropping to 13°C in the daytime and 7°C at night. The most rain falls in November so along with the cold it can be very wet as well.

Occasionally some of the days of autumn can be pleasant enough to go out in short sleeves but the sea will be very cold. December to February is not really cold but is certainly chilly; the average high is 11°C which goes down to a low of 4°C. Around the coastal areas snow and frost are extremely rare but the sky can be very grey, with only occasional sunshine.

Sights & Activities: What to See & Do

Biarritz

Napoleon III chose this little fishing port to build a summer residence for Empress Eugénie in the middle of the 19th century. The villa he built for her in the shape of a letter E was converted into a hotel in 1893 and is now the Hôtel

BIARRITZ TRAVEL GUIDE

du Palais. Biarritz had always been a popular tourist destination known for its spas and thalassotherapy but the construction of the casino in 1901 made doubly sure it was on the must-see list of the rich and well-to-do. Biarritz is a very cosmopolitan city compared to the rest of the French Basque country and has been influenced by many styles from art deco to Russian.

Biarritz town centre is best explored on foot as driving can be stressful in the hilly, one-way streets. Take a stroll along the promenade to blow the cobwebs away and then seek shelter in the Old Town for a well-deserved café au lait. Head across Place Sainte Eugenie towards Rue des Halles to where the market traders line the streets and find a little bar or café to sit and watch the world pass by.

History Museum

Rue Broquedis

64200 Biarritz

Tel: +33 559 248 628

The museum is a good place to start off and learn about the history of Biarritz. In a building that used to be an Anglican church the museum was set up in 1986 by a group of people who wanted to revive the city's past. As Napoleon III has strong ties with Biarritz there are many references and memorials to the part he played in the both the town and the war. Just inside the door there is the Bonaparte family tree. A wide collection of subjects can be found including photographs from the 1920's, lists of people who died in the Napoleonic wars and information on Queen Victoria's visit.

BIARRITZ TRAVEL GUIDE

There is memorabilia from the imperial family including jewelry, medals and flags representing military history. The museum is open Tuesday to Saturday from 10am to 12.30pm and 2.30pm to 6.30pm. Admission for adults is €4, there are reductions for students with children under 10 are admitted free.

Virgin on the Rock

Biarritz

The Virgin on the Rock is the statue that is said to protect the fishermen and sailors in the Bay of Biscay. The statue perched on her rocky islet can be reached by crossing the footbridge designed by Gustav Eiffel of Eiffel Tower fame. Don't worry though; although the ironwork might look familiar the footbridge is much lower. The walk across can be quite dramatic with the waves crashing onto the rocks below but it is invigorating with the salty smell of the sea in the fresh air.

Museum of the Sea

Plateau de l'Atalaye

Rocher de la Vierge

64200 Biarritz

Tel: +33 559 223 334

www.museedelamer.com/

The Museum of the Sea was first opened in 1933 and has been extended and renovated over the years so that visitors can explore the Caribbean Sea, the Gulf Stream and the Indo-Pacific region. The footprint of the museum has increased from 3,500m^2 to 7,000m^2 with fifty aquariums housing thousands of species and one of the largest pools in France at 1,500m^2.

There are sharks and seals aplenty in the sea museum. Seal-feeding time will delight children and there is a touchy-feely pool to get to know these underwater creatures better. The museum is open November to March from 9.30am until 7pm, July and August 9.30am until midnight and all the other months are 9.30am until 8pm. Adults, €13.50, children €9.50 and a family ticket is €48.

City of the Ocean

1 avenue de la Plage, la Milady

64200 Biarritz

Tel: +33 559 227 540

BIARRITZ TRAVEL GUIDE

www.citedelocean.com

The more modern Ocean City in Biarritz has 3D Pop-out technology and interactive experiences. Join in with the refloating of a sunken ship and listen to Christopher Columbus tell tales about his adventures. Learn about the oceans, the climate and mankind and see why explorers for hundreds of years have been fascinated by the polar regions. Admission prices are €10.50 per adult, €7 for a child and €37 for a family ticket. Opening times are varied so it is best to check the website before you visit.

Asiatic and Oriental Art Museum

1 Rue Guy Petit

64200 Biarritz

BIARRITZ TRAVEL GUIDE

Tel: +33 559 227 878

www.museeasiatica.com/

If you don't have time to visit the Far East this museum has more than enough exhibits to satisfy your curiosity. There are permanent collections from Nepal, China, India and Tibet with over 1,000 objects spread out over two levels as well as temporary collections ranging from paintings and poetry to photography.

A guidebook is lent to each visitor to explain about the different exhibits and audio-guides are available to rent. The museum is open every day from 2pm until 6.30pm with extended hours in July and August. Admission price is €10 for adults with discounts for under 25's. Entry to the temporary exhibitions is free.

BIARRITZ TRAVEL GUIDE

Biarritz Lighthouse

Pointe St Martin

Biarritz

The lighthouse at Biarritz was built in 1834 and stands in prettily manicured gardens which are lovely to walk through to enjoy the views. There are benches in the gardens and it is a lovely place to take a picnic. Make an effort to go to the top of the 73-metre lighthouse. There are about 250 steps to climb and you will be rewarded with amazing views of the town, the Basque coast all the way to Spain.

If you happen to be there on Bastille Day there will be stalls in the gardens where you can buy food and drink and mingle with the locals. The entry fee is €2.50 and there are toilet facilities available in the nearby building.

🌍 Bayonne

The areas history can be traced back to when the city of Bayonne was called Lapurdum after the occupation of the Romans. The name change to Bayonne didn't come until the 11th century. Six hundred years ago Bayonne was a busy port which was first developed by the English. Today Bayonne is the centre of regional government in the French Basque country as well as a tourist destination but hangs on to its old world charm in an endearing fashion.

The winding streets are full of tiny bars that will serve you a Kir in the afternoon sun and restaurants selling the famous jambon de Bayonne. The ham is locally cured and seasoned with the Espelette red peppers grown in the region. For anyone with a sweet tooth Bayonne could be the ideal place to holiday as chocolate making is a thriving industry.

The tradition dates back to the 16th century when Portuguese and Spanish Jews fled to France during the Spanish Inquisition. A two day festival in May, Les Journées du Chocolat de Bayonne, sees the town centre overtaken by chocoholics as free samples and goodies are handed out. Don't miss out on the chocolate mousse from Cazenave; this foamy hot chocolate has the most scrumptious taste ever.

In July every year the town comes to life with the Bayonne Festival. Dating back to 1932 this event is one of the biggest in France. The crowds dress in white with red sashes and kerchiefs and the town comes to life.

BIARRITZ TRAVEL GUIDE

Bullfights, concerts, street parades, fun and games all take place in the streets over the four day period accompanied by plenty of drinking and eating.

Cazenave Chocolate Shop & Tea Room

19 Arceaux Port Neuf

64100 Bayonne

Tel: +33 559 590 316

www.chocolats-bayonne-cazenave.fr/

The history of Cazenave chocolate began in 1854 when Martin Pierre Cazenave aged just 22 started making his delicious sweet treats. Cazenave is now owned and run by the grandchildren of the original waitress in the tearoom.

The tearoom was created in the early 20th century from the old adjoining workshop and decorated in the characteristic décor of the time. That elegance still exists and you can drink tea, or chocolate, from Limoges china beautifully presented on individual trays.

The stained glass windows and decorated woodwork and mirrors hark back to a long gone era. The tearoom and shop is open Tuesday to Saturday from 9.15am to midday and from 2pm until 7pm. In the school holidays you can also visit on Mondays.

Saint Mary's Cathedral & Cloister

15 Rue des Prébendes

64100 Bayonne

BIARRITZ TRAVEL GUIDE

Tel: +33 559 591 782

www.bayonne-tourisme.com/

Saint Mary's cathedral is on a slight rise in the heart of Bayonne overlooking the Adour and Nive rivers. The Gothic style cathedral was built from local stone on the site of a Romanesque cathedral that in 1258 was destroyed by fire. Most of the construction was done between the 13th and 16th centuries but the 85 metre high twin spires were not completed until the 19th century thanks to the determination of Boeswillwald.

The stained glass windows are done in the style of Chartres cathedral and the chapels are decorated paintings by Steinhel. The cathedral contains relics of a 9th century Bishop of Bayonne, Saint Leo and in 1998 was listed as a World Heritage Site.

BIARRITZ TRAVEL GUIDE

The adjoining cloister dates back to 1240 and is one of the largest in France. The stained glass windows show scenes from the Old and New testaments and through the Middle Ages it was used as a cemetery. For many centuries this has been a place to stop for pilgrims walking to St Jean Pied de Port. The cathedral and cloister are open Monday to Friday 10am to 11.45am and 3pm to 6.45pm, Saturdays 10am to 11.45am and 3pm to 5.45pm and Sundays 3pm to 6.45pm. Admission is free.

History Museum of the Basques

37 Quai des Corsaires

64100 Bayonne

Tél. +33 559 590 898

www.musee-basque.com/

BIARRITZ TRAVEL GUIDE

Three floors and twenty rooms or so in the setting of Dagourette House will reveal the richness of Basque history. There is so much to see in here with 2,000 objects covering many subjects including dancing and the fandango, mythology, architecture and Basque pelote. Inside the museum there is a reconstructed typical Basque home and a farm. This makes it easy to explore and understand the cultural identity, traditions and seafaring history of the Basque people.

Everything is labelled in French, Basque and Spanish but leaflets are available in English. The museum is open from 10am until 6.30pm, closed Mondays, and an adult ticket costs €5.50 and children get in free.

Bonnat Museum

5 rue Jacques Lafitte

64100 Bayonne

Tel: +33 559 590 852

www.museebonnat.bayonne.fr

In 1901 a local man, Léon Bonnat, gave his collection of art and drawings to the City of Bayonne and over the years the collection has grown thanks to the gifts of art from other donors. The Bonnat Museum has an impressive art collection and the drawings it houses are the finest collection outside of the Louvre. There are 6500 exhibits including 3500 drawings by Sandro Botticelli, Le Lorrain, Michelangelo, Giulio Romano, Primaticcio, Raphael, Charles Le Brun and approximately 30 other famous names.

BIARRITZ TRAVEL GUIDE

There are works by El Greco, Bartolomé Esteban Murillo, Thomas Lawrence, Francisco de Goya, Van Dyck, Rembrandt, Joshua Reynolds, John Constable, J.M.W. Turner and Rubens. The 19th century French masters are represented by Degas, Boudin, Puvis de Chavannes, Corot, Courbet, David, Delacroix, Géricault, Girodet, Ingres, and Bonnat himself. To see these unexpected treasures the museum is open Wednesday through to Monday from 10am until 6.30pm. Children get in free and adults pay €5.50

🌎 Saint Jean-de-Luz

St.-Jean-de-Luz is a pretty fishing community set around a picturesque horseshoe bay with a road leading up into the mountains. Wealth first came to the town from the fishing and whaling industries then the exploits of the

BIARRITZ TRAVEL GUIDE

Basque Corsairs (pirates) added to the crown's purse by capturing foreign ships. Of course the piracy and whaling days are over but the fishing still goes on. The best place to find eateries and sample this delicious fresh fish is along Rue de la République.

Avoid the more hectic pace of Biarritz at the tranquil St.-Jean-de-Luz with its protected beaches and vast stretches of sand and calm waters for swimming. In the summer months the little tourist train is an ideal way of having a tour of the town without wearing yourself out. If you are ready for a sit down and a drink find one of the many bars round the Place Louis XIV. This is a pretty square in the town where you can often find traditional music being played by local musicians.

BIARRITZ TRAVEL GUIDE

This vibrant and cosmopolitan town has everything for a super holiday. With a lush green backdrop of the surrounding countryside the town has markets and festivals aplenty, the beaches are clean and safe and there are many activities to choose from whether land or sea based. It is an excellent family destination with something to do for everyone.

Saint John the Baptist Church

Rue Gambetta,

64500 Saint-Jean-de-Luz

Tel: +33 559 260 881

The angular exterior doesn't give any clue to the spectacular sights inside this church. It is the largest Basque church in France and well worth a visit. The altarpiece is impressive, a vision in gold and used in 1660 at the marriage of the French king to Maria Teresa, a Spanish princess, took place in St.-Jean-de-Luz in the incredibly beautiful church of St-Jean-Baptiste. Once the wedding had taken place the doorway to the church was blocked up, thus ensuring no one else could pass through it.

House of Louis XIV

6 Place Louis XIV

64500 Saint-Jean-de-Luz

Tel+33 559 260 156

www.maison-louis-xiv.fr/

The house of Louis XIV was built by Joannis de Lohobiague, a shipowner, in 1643 and is still lived in as a private residence and belongs to the same family that built it. The house is in a pretty square where there are

BIARRITZ TRAVEL GUIDE

numerous cafés and plenty of trees for shade in the summer. The street is close to the quayside and there is plenty of parking nearby.

Inside the house you start off by climbing two flights of wooden stairs so this is unfortunately not a visit for disabled people. The house is where the 22 year old Louis XIV waited for 40 days for his young bride, also 22, to arrive from Spain. The rooms are richly decorated with colourful walls and rich soft furnishings and might be a little overpowering for today's more minimalist taste.

The house is open from April to November, but closed every Tuesday. The guided tours are at 11am, 3pm and 4pm with extra times in the height of the summer. The admission price is €6 for adults and €3.50 for children between 12 and 18.

BIARRITZ TRAVEL GUIDE

🌍 St.-Jean-Pied-de-Port

St.-Jean-Pied-de-Port sits just north of the Roncevaux Pass and is the last stop on the Santiago de Compostela pilgrimage route. The pass itself is entirely in Spain and is at a height of 1,057 metres. One of the most attractive towns in the French Basque country, St.-Jean-Pied-de-Port sits high up in the hills and can be reached by train from Bayonne. The journey takes about an hour and for most of the way the track runs alongside the fast flowing river.

The town was named after Saint James in the New Testament after his remains were supposedly discovered in Santiago de Compostela in Spain. This all happened over a thousand years ago and ever since then pilgrims have flocked from Northern Europe to Spain through St.-

BIARRITZ TRAVEL GUIDE

Jean-Pied-de-Port and through the notoriously difficult Roncevaux Pass.

The pilgrims do still come from the north and can be seen in traditional dress of sandals and long brown cloaks trudging along the dusty roads. However, most visitors to St.-Jean-Pied-de-Port are usually quite happy to wander round the town and watch the local playing Basque pelota against a pink wall.

Cheese Cave

2, Place des Remparts

64220 Saint Jean Pied de Port

Tel: +33 559 491 031

www.fromage-brebis.com/

Saint Jean Pied de Port is famous for its sheep's cheese or Ossaulraty. The village is in the heart of sheep-farming country so access to the main ingredient is easy! The cheeses are made from both raw and treated milk for different strength and flavours and then left to mature for up to four months. After learning about the history of the cheese-making process there is a tasting session at the end of the tour. It is free to visit the cheese factory and opening times are 9am until12 noon and 2pm until 6pm.

Bishop's Prison

41 rue de la Citadelle

64220 Saint-Jean-Pied-De-Port

Tel: +33 559 370 092

In the Bishop's Prison there are permanent and temporary exhibitions are on display to help visitors understand

BIARRITZ TRAVEL GUIDE

Basque culture and history. Displays include Templar gear and costumes and artefacts from olden times. The building was not actually used as a prison when the Bishop of Avignon was controlling the area in the 13th century but did become the town jail hundreds of years later.

It was also used through the Second World War as an internment camp and at times for storing military goods. The prison is open from March through to November. In the earlier and later months there is an afternoon break but in the height of the season the museum is open all day. Adults pay €3 and children under 14 years of age are admitted free.

🌍 Route de Corniche (between Saint-Jean-de-Luz & Hendaye)

The Route de Corniche is the coast road that runs from Saint-Jean-de-Luz and Ciboure to Hendaye. The road stretches for 19 kilometres staying close to the rocky coast in some parts and in others through verdant green pastures.

Starting in St-Jean-de-Luz and passing through Ciboure there is a glorious drive, or walk, across the Cornishe de Socoa cliffs. Ciboure is the birthplace of Maurice Ravel, born in 1875 and the composer of the Bolero made famous in the 1984 Winter Olympics.

As you get closer to Hendaye look out for Chateau Abbadia, a stunning chateau that is open to the public. Pointe Ste-Anne is a short walk down the cliff below

Chateau Abbadia and offers unrivalled views over the Golfe de Gascogne.

The descent into Hendaye takes you right down to the beach where the Route de Corniche joins the Boulevard de le Mer and takes you down to the port. Hendaye is right on the French-Spanish border and the Bay of Chingoudy separates the two countries. The 3.5 kilometre beach here is the longest beach on the Basque coast.

🌍 Little Train of La Rhune

Sare, 64320

Tel: +33 559 542 026

www.rhune.com

If you are a lover of speed then the Little Train of La Rhune might not be for you! The little wooden train will

BIARRITZ TRAVEL GUIDE

take you at the gentle pace of just nine kilometres per hour up to the top of La Rhune mountain to a height of 905 metres. The summit of the La Rhune mountain is right on the border between France and Spain but the railway is completely in the Pyrénées-Atlantiques department of France.

The train line to the top of the mountain was first planned in 1908 and work started in 1912 but this was stopped by World War I. The line eventually opened many years later in 1924. In 1978 the villagers voted against a road being built up to the top of the mountain and so the train survived.

The four-wheeled locomotive is powered by electric and pushes the two coaches up and leads them down the mountain. The trains run every 35 minutes from mid-

March to early November and can carry up to 120 passengers at a time. The fare is like the mountain, steep, at €18 but the journey is well worth the cost. Train times vary according to the month so check before you travel.

🌍 Villa Arnaga House & Gardens

Villa Arnaga - Musée Edmond Rostand

Route du Docteur Camino

64250 Cambo-les-Bains

Tel +33 559 298 392

www.arnaga.com/

Villa Arnaga is located in the heart of the Basque country 15 kilometres from both Bayonne and Biarritz. The villa and gardens were created by Edmond Rostand, an author and poet, who was born in April 1868 in Marseilles. Rostand decided to set up home in Cambo-les-Bains and

BIARRITZ TRAVEL GUIDE

with the help of a Parisian architect, Albert Tournaire, the sketches he had made materialised into detailed plans.

The house was built between 1903 and 1906. The exterior of the villa is very much in the Basque style with the typical white painted walls and the timbers stained ox-blood red. The gardens cover 17 hectares and are immaculate and designed in different styles. The peace and tranquility of these carefully planned spaces is disturbed only by the tinkling of the fountains and it is easy to drift off and imagine yourself in the France of a century ago.

The inside of the villa is stunning with beautifully decorated and hand-painted walls and ceilings, elegant galleries and intricate wooden panelling. The antichamber is a small oval room that was used for storing clothes and is a far cry from the fitted wardrobes of today.

Choosing your outfit would have been a pleasure in this room decorated from floor to ceiling with Chinese inspired drawings in ochre tones using the camaïeu technique. Rostand was very forward thinking and even installed his own sauna and hydrotherapy room. The white and blue tiles give a simplistic design to the room and by using a combination of lead foil and wood the steam created by the boiling water diffused throughout the room creating the sauna effect.

The bookcases and shelves are full of original works by Rostand and other poets, authors and cartoonists of the time. An adult ticket to see all these inspiring works is €7 with reductions for students and children. The house is open from April 1st until October 31st and the daily times vary, so maybe check the website first. There are various events and demonstrations held at Villa Arnaga such as theatre nights, nighttime garden visits and concerts so check to see what is on before you go.

🌍 Grottos of Isturitz & Oxocelhaya

Saint Martin d'Arberoue,

64640 Bayonne

Tel: +33 559 296 472

www.grottes-isturitz.com/

Take a drive an hour inland from the Basque coast to Saint Martin d'Arberoue you will find the caves of Oxocelhaya. After you have driven through the pretty countryside and admired the typical Basque farm

BIARRITZ TRAVEL GUIDE

buildings the caves are an easy ten minute walk up the hillside from the free car park.

The Caves of Oxocelhaya date back to the middle part of the Stone Age and there is evidence of Neanderthal man living there. The caves themselves are home to the most amazing stalactites and stalagmites plus carvings and cave paintings. One of the best parts is the column decorated with animal carvings from thousands of years ago.

There is a guided 45 minute tour and although it is in French there are printed cards in English and Spanish to help you understand what the guide is saying. The tours are fairly frequent throughout the day and even if you have just missed one there is a pleasant café, a shop and an exhibition about the caves to pass the time. The caves

BIARRITZ TRAVEL GUIDE

are open from March 5th until November 15th and adult ticket costs €9.50. Children's tickets are €4 but there is a family ticket at €28 which is good value for two adults and up to three children.

🌐 Basque Cake Museum

Maison Haranea - Quartier Lehenbiscaye

64310 Sare

Tel: +33 559 542 209

www.legateaubasque.com/

If you love cakes and Basque food then a day out to this museum will be ideal. The Gateau Basque is a filled cake and you can usually tell the filling by the pattern on top of the cake. A crosshatch pattern indicates a cream filling while a Basque cross decoration means black cherry jam.

BIARRITZ TRAVEL GUIDE

There are different tours available and in the shorter tour the pastry chef demonstrates in front of you how to make and cook the cake. Other tours can involve hands-on baking as you make your own cake plus lunch with traditional Basque food.

There is a restaurant as well as shop and the Basque biscuits are a very popular and delicious choice to buy. The museum is about 2 kilometres from Sare and is a bit tricky to find but well worth the effort The shop and museum is open Monday to Friday from 9.30am until 6pm. Tour prices start at €7.50 up to €33.

🌐 Chateau Abbadia

Route de la Corniche

64700 Hendaye

Tel: +33 559 200 451

BIARRITZ TRAVEL GUIDE

www.chateau-abbadia.fr/

Chateau Abbadia sits on the cliffs just north of Hendaye and has spectacular views of the Atlantic Ocean and the Basque coastline. The chateau was built in the fifteen year period from 1864 to 1879 by the architect Eugène Viollet-le-Duc at the request of Antoine d'Abbadie.

An outstanding scholar who loved astronomy, oriental culture and geography d'Abbadie also had a great love of all things Basque. The gardens surrounding the chateau were designed by Eugène Buhlerand and are planted with many palm trees and are a pleasure to walk through.

The building has been cleverly designed to look like a castle and there are towers and battlements galore. Look out for the many stone animals decorating the walls outside, there are cats chasing mice as well as monkeys, snakes and elephants.

d'Abbadie had a passion for all things oriental and was also very interested in science and after an 11 year stay in Ethiopia started drawing maps not just of the land but of the night skies as well. These passions are highlighted in the decoration and furnishings inside the chateau.

The highly polished wooden floors reflect the brightly coloured furnishings and the most amazing ceilings decorated in straight lines. One of the bedrooms was specially created for Napoleon III and the library with its galleried bookshelves holds many scientific publications and machines from the days when there was an observatory in the chateau.

From 1871-1875 he was Mayor of Hendaye and he was given the honorary title of Father of the Basque people when he died. The death of d'Abbadie in 1897 was of benefit to the Academy of Sciences to whom he bequeathed his chateau and they still own it today. The astronomical observatory finally stopped operating in 1979. Admission prices for adults are €7 to €8 and for children €3 to €4. The opening times and days vary widely through the year, so check the website or ask at the local tourist information office first.

La-Pierre-St-Martin Ski Resort

www.lapierrestmartin.com/

The ski resort of La-Pierre-St-Martin is in the Barétous valley between the Spanish Pyrénées and Béarn. The

BIARRITZ TRAVEL GUIDE

resort has four airports within three hours drive so access is good. Lourdes and Pau are about two hours' drive, Huesca is an hour and half and Zaragoza is three hours.

The skiing takes place at over 2000 metres so snowfall is pretty reliable but if not there are 55 snow cannons. The 13 ski lifts give access to 20 pistes and can uplift 11,000 people per hour. There are runs to suit all abilities but intermediate skiers will probably benefit most. With a season ticket for just €69 for adults and €31 for children it has all the benefits of the more well known resorts without the price tag.

Any non-skiers in the family can have fun in the snow as well as there are guided snowshoe walks, tandem-ski rides with the ski instructors and sledging. When you get tired of all the activities, how about a good old-fashioned

BIARRITZ TRAVEL GUIDE

snowball fight? Away from the snow there is table tennis and squash if you have any energy left. Each week the tourist office displays the programme of events. There can be torch-lit ski descents, mulled wine tastings, firework displays, snow Olympics and ski displays by the instructors.

La-Pierre-St-Martin village is very aware that handicapped people still like to experience the thrill of the snow and the La Pierre Handiski Pyrénées is a recognised association for motor, mental and visual handicaps. Most of the lifts and slopes are accessible and the staff is trained to assist. There are modern apartment blocks to stay in or little wooden chalets hiding under the fir trees. There are of course shops, bars and restaurants so all you have to do is ski and have fun.

Etxola Animal Park

Route des Grottes - Route de Lizarrieta

64310 Sare

Tel: +33 615 068 951

www.etxola-parc-animalier.com/

Etxola Animal Park was created in 1999 and there are many rare breed domestic animals here from all over the world. Lots of these breeds are forgotten about or fast disappearing and the park is trying to keep them from dying out. Many of the smaller animals are roaming free and it is a great opportunity to let children get up close and personal with some furry or feathered friends. There are lots of birds, some easily recognisable like chickens and pigeons and some unfamiliar animals as well.

BIARRITZ TRAVEL GUIDE

There are several varieties of cows, some with enormously long horns and some with ruffles of fur round their necks and Brahman cattle with weird humps on their necks. There are camels, llamas, pigs and deer to keep you entertained as you walk along the shady path through this animal park in the heart of the mountains. Extola is open from March 23rd until November 11th and an adult ticket is €5 with children paying just €4. The park opens at 10am until 6pm with slightly later closing in the summer months.

BIARRITZ TRAVEL GUIDE

Budget Tips

Accommodation

Maison E. Bernat

20 rue de la Citadelle

64220 Saint-Jean-Pied-de-Port

Tel: +33 559 372 310

BIARRITZ TRAVEL GUIDE

www.ebernat.com/

This guesthouse is right in the heart of the medieval town centre of Saint-Jean-Pied-de-Port. There is a lot of history in the house, which was built in 1662 and the garden offers outstanding views and leads up to the walls of the fortress in the city centre.

The three comfortably appointed bedrooms are named after local areas and can sleep up to three people. All the rooms have one double and one single bed and have a private bathroom.

The rooms are priced between €70 and €90 depending on season for two people sharing; a third person is an extra €26 regardless of season. The room price includes breakfast with homemade preserves, freshly baked breads and pastries, cheeses and a choice of hot and cold drinks. There is also a small restaurant serving locally sourced produce and there are set menus to try starting at €20.

Quick Palace Anglet

2 Avenue de Cambo

64600, Anglet

Tel. +33 559 314 272

www.quickpalace.fr

This budget hotel is only a couple of kilometres from Biarritz Airport and five kilometres from the beach. There is free parking and the Makila Golf Club is close by. There are 59 soundproofed rooms with private bathrooms; they all have flat-screen TV with satellite channels and a work desk with free Wifi access. The reception is open 24 hours a day and a buffet breakfast is available. Prices start at €49 per person per night.

Manoir Théas

Rd 936

64390 Barraute Camu

Tel: +33 559 385 734

www.manoir-theas.com

Manoir Théas is in a beautiful area halfway between the Pyrénées and the Atlantic Ocean. The five bedrooms are all individually decorated with polished wooden floors and period furniture but with the technology of flat-screen TV. All the rooms have private bathrooms. In the summer guests can enjoy breakfast on the terrace and there is a swimming pool and deckchairs are available.

BIARRITZ TRAVEL GUIDE

A communal kitchen and lounge are there for guests to use and the hosts speak English if your French hasn't improved since your schooldays! The river is only 200 metres away and there are plenty of outdoor activities like fishing, hiking and horseriding. There is one suite and four bedrooms each with a bath or shower. Prices start from €40 per person per night if three or four guests share a room or €48 per person per night for one or two guests. An extra bed is €10.

Hotel Club Vacanciel Salies de Bearn

4, Avenue al Cartero

64720, Salies-de-Béarn

Tel: +33 559 387 300

www.vacanciel.com/

BIARRITZ TRAVEL GUIDE

This smart hotel has all you need for a holiday in the area between the Pyrénées and the Basque coast. The hotel sits in three acres of lawned grounds with beautifully kept trees providing shade when the sun gets too much.

There is a swimming pool with plenty of room to sunbathe and deckchairs for an afternoon nap. If you feel a bit more energetic there is a tennis court and a games room and for the little ones a children's playground. There is a small shop where you can buy local products and gifts.

Breakfast is served daily in Le Biharnou restaurant and in the evenings a selection of traditional French meals are served. Free Wifi access is available in the hotel bar so

BIARRITZ TRAVEL GUIDE

you can enjoy a drink while catching up with friends back home.

There are some organised events for guests with regional food tastings, volleyball competitions and entertainment in the evening. There is free parking at the hotel and a shuttle bus runs between the hotel and the train station in Puyoo.

The comfortable rooms can sleep between one and four guests and there are disabled friendly rooms available for guests with special needs. Prices are from €55 per person depending on the season but there are various special offers and meal deals to be found on the website.

Hotel Uhainak

3, Boulevard de la Mer

64700, Hendaye

Tel: +33 559 203 363

www.hotel-uhainak.com/

BIARRITZ TRAVEL GUIDE

The Hotel Uhainak is only steps away from the wide, sandy beach where you can walk uninterrupted for around three kilometres gazing across the Atlantic Ocean.

As the hotel is so close to the sea all the rooms are double-glazed to keep the elements out and they all have television, telephone and private bathroom. Breakfast is available and is served in the dining room where there are panoramic views across the sea. There are 14 rooms, one being approved for disabled guests and prices vary depending on season, which floor they are on and how many beds. Starting at €52 the prices go up to €116.

Restaurants, Cafés & Bars

Chez Mattin

Place de la Croix Rouge

64500 Ciboure

Tel: +33 559 471 952

Chez Mattin is a highly regarded restaurant on the

Basque coast. The cosy restaurant is decorated with pictures, statues and plenty of interesting objects to admire while enjoying your meal.

The locals use Chez Mattin all the time and you can't get a better recommendation that that. Tucked away down a side street and a few hundred metres from the marina, Chez Mattin serves excellent fish dishes. Try the calamari or the locally caught merluza, but if you don't fancy fish there are plenty of other choices and the duck comes highly recommended. The staff are friendly and attentive and prices start at €25.

Auberge Du Petit Bayonne

23, Rue des Cordeliers

64100 Bayonne, France

Tel: +33 559 598 344

BIARRITZ TRAVEL GUIDE

www.auberge-du-petit-bayonne.fr/

Close to the river in the beautiful town of Bayonne is Auberge du Petit Bayonne. The hosts Cathy and Eric are welcoming and you will soon relax in the friendly atmosphere. The feature stone wall and wooden panelling give the restaurant a cosy, homely feel. They serve high quality Basque cuisine at reasonable prices and the daily menu starts at just €11.50. The menu has a wide selection including lamb, duck and fish dishes, all prepared to the highest standards.

Bar Jean

5, rue de Halles,

64200 Biarritz

Tel: +33 559 248 038

BIARRITZ TRAVEL GUIDE

www.barjean-biarritz.com/

In one of the little streets near the Biarritz market is Bar Jean. The bar has been serving delicious Basque pintxos and meals to locals and tourists for over 30 years. The small terrace outside with a few chairs and tables is small but inside the restaurant is quite big. The decor is a mix of old and new, formica topped tables with old wooden chairs are ideal for two people while tile-topped tables and wooden benches are great for groups of friends.

To sample Basque cuisine try some of the pintxos, bite-sized nibbles served on a cocktail stick. Each one is €1 so you can fill your plate with these or have a few as a starter before trying maybe the Côte de boeuf as a main course. There is a daily menu starting at €9 as well as the á la carte. The restaurant is popular and is open for meals all day. Everyone is welcome, including families and four-legged friends.

Restaurant les Trois Fontaines

Col De St Ignace

64310 Sare

Tel: +33 559 542 080

The Restaurant le Trois Fontaines sits in a beautiful garden filled with shrubs and flowers with a backdrop of vibrant green trees. The garden is child-friendly and there are swings and slides to keep the children amused.

The pretty white painted building has a rustic dining room and a terrace overlooking the stunning scenery for eating al fresco in the summer months. If you don't fancy driving through the French countryside the famous train of Rhune stops at the station very close to the restaurant. The restaurant is open from March until November and the daily menu starts at €11.50 with a children's menu at €7.

Ttotta

Espace Ibarrondoan RD 918,

64310 Saint-Pee-sur-Nivelle

Tel: +33 559 470 355

www.ttotta.fr/

Ttotta is a family run restaurant in a modern setting but the food is in traditional Basque style. The restaurant is bright with light wooden furniture and the pale grey table linen gives the dining area a fresh look. Children are welcome and the homemade Tottaburger with freshly cut chips is a world apart from your usual burger and fries. Main courses start from €16 and there is a splendid range of fish, meat and fowl to choose from, but if you are not sure what to choose there is a daily menu for €13.

🌍 Shopping

Bayonne Markets

www.bayonne-commerces.com/

Markets are one of the best places to see the local color of a town and Bayonne has more than its fair share. Markets operate most days of the week and open around 7am. From fruit to fish, fair trade to organic farming there is a huge choice.

There are old clothes, new clothes and locally produced cheeses, breads and cakes. Second-hand dealers with furniture, painting and antiques will try to tempt you into buying what maybe the find of the century. Some of the most popular markets are:

Les Halles

Every morning from Monday to Friday from 7am to 1.30pm, Saturday from 6am to 1.30pm and Sunday from 8am to 1.30pm.

Place de la République, Saint Esprit area

Every Friday from 7am to 1pm.

Rue Sainte Catherine, Saint Esprit

Every Sunday from 8am to Midday.

Place du Marquisat, bd jean d'Amou

Every Friday from 8am to 1pm.

BIARRITZ TRAVEL GUIDE

Place des Gascons, Hauts de Sainte Croix

Every Wednesday and Saturday 7am to 1pm.

Polo Beyris

Every Friday from 7am to 1pm.

Flea market Carreau des Halles

Every Friday 7am to 1pm.

Saint-Jean-de-Luz

Rue Gambetta

The main shopping street of St.-Jean-de-Luz is pedestrianised so you can shop to your heart's content without being run over by a mad driver in a Citroën. The street runs parallel to the beach and is packed with historical buildings and tiny little shops selling traditional products and handmade articles. Rue Gambetta is lined with typical Basque style houses with brightly coloured shutters and geraniums tumbling down from nearly every windowsill.

Pau-Pyrenees

www.pau-pyrenees.com/

The town of Pau has many different areas for shopping and there are so many shops that you can even take a guided tour, in French, round them. The Castle District with its pedestrian roads is filled with souvenir shops and antiques dealers surrounded by restaurants and bars.

You can stroll down the wide pavements of Bosquet Avenue and the road of Cordeliers and the Samonzet and Serviez roads are close by if you get bored. The Bosquet shopping centre has 40 shops for you to explore and was opened in 1991. For shopping in a chic style Foch, Barthou or Joffre roads offer brand names in ready-to-wear clothes and fashion accessories. In the Lescar area surrounded by a beautiful tropical garden is the Quartier Libre shopping centre.

Accoceberry

Rue principale

64250 Espelette

Tel +33 559 938 649

www.accoceberry.fr/

The Espelette red pepper is famous in the French Basque country and there is nowhere better to buy some than in the village of the same name. In 1959 Jean Accoceberry opened a butchers shop in his home village. By 2004 the family business had expanded to shops, warehouses and a banquet hall offering a range of 80 different products all to do with the medium-spiced pepper.

There are gourmet hampers to choose from, other tempting products include foie gras, tripe, desserts, sauces and piquillos. How about trying the Graisserons. These are fatty and lean bits of meat, pork or duck, mixed roughly with all their flavour caught in the gravy. Served cold as a starter or served warm in an omelette they are delicious.

Ainciart-Bergara

64 480 Larressore

Tel: +33 559 930 305

www.makhila.com

BIARRITZ TRAVEL GUIDE

The traditional French basque walking stick called the mahkila is often copied and sold in tourist shops but for the genuine article take a trip to Larressore, 15 kilometres from Bayonne. Here in the workshop you can see the time-honoured methods that go into the making of this sturdy walking companion. For over 200 years the mahkila has been made by the Ainciart family since Dominique Ainciart was born in 1796.

The walking sticks are made from the rare medlar tree in the springtime. The desired decorations are cut into the chosen branch while it is still on the tree. In winter the branch is cut from the tree when the various marks and grooves have had time to expand.

The drying period is several years after which the mahkila is painted with a secret recipe and decorated. Family crests, mottos, and any manner of decorations can be added at the customer's request. You can be sure that your mahkila will be unique to you and your family.

BIARRITZ TRAVEL GUIDE

Know Before You Go

🌍 Entry Requirements

By virtue of the Schengen agreement, visitors from other countries in the European Union will not need a visa when visiting France. Additionally Swiss visitors are also exempt. Visitors from certain other countries such as Andorra, Canada, the United Kingdom, Ireland, the Bahamas, Australia, the USA, Chile, Costa Rica, Croatia, El Salvador, Guatemala, Honduras, Israel, Malaysia, Mauritius, Monaco, Nicaragua, New Zealand, Panama, Paraguay, Saint Kitts and Nevis, San Marino, the Holy See, Seychelles, Taiwan and Japan do not need visas for a stay of less than 90 days. Visitors to France must be in possession of a valid passport that expires no sooner than three months after the intended stay. UK citizens will not need a visa to enter France. Visitors must provide proof of residence, financial support and the reason for their visit. If you wish to work or study in France, however, you will need a visa.

Health Insurance

Citizens of other EU countries are covered for emergency health care in France. UK residents, as well as visitors from Switzerland are covered by the European Health Insurance Card (EHIC), which can be applied for free of charge. Visitors from non-Schengen countries will need to show proof of private health insurance that is valid for the duration of their stay in France (that offers at least €37,500 coverage), as part of their visa application. A letter of coverage will need to be submitted to the French Embassy along with your visa application. American travellers will need to check whether their regular medical insurance covers international travel. No special vaccinations are required.

Travelling with Pets

France participates in the Pet Travel Scheme (PETS) which allows UK residents to travel with their pets without requiring quarantine upon re-entry. Certain conditions will need to be met. The animal will have to be microchipped and up to date on rabies vaccinations. In the case of dogs, France also requires vaccination against distemper. If travelling from another EU member country, you will need an EU pet passport. Regardless of the country, a Declaration of Non-Commercial Transport must be signed stating that you do not intend to sell your pet.

BIARRITZ TRAVEL GUIDE

A popular form of travel with pets between the UK and France is via the Eurotunnel, which has special facilities for owners travelling with pets. This includes dedicated pet exercise areas and complimentary dog waste bags. Transport of a pet via this medium costs €24. The Calais Terminal has a special Pet Reception Building. Pets travelling from the USA will need to be at least 12 weeks old and up to date on rabies vaccinations. Microchipping or some form of identification tattoo will also be required. If travelling from another country, do inquire about the specific entry requirements for your pet into France and also about re-entry requirements in your own country.

🌏 Airports

There are three airports near Paris where most international visitors arrive. The largest of these is **Charles De Gaulle** (CDG) airport, which serves as an important hub for both international and domestic carriers. It is located about 30km outside Paris and is well-connected to the city's rail network. Most trans-Atlantic flights arrive here. **Orly** (ORY) is the second largest and oldest airport serving Paris. It is located 18km south of the city and is connected to several public transport options including a bus service, shuttle service and Metro rail. Most of its arrivals and departures are to other destinations within Europe. **Aéroport de Paris-Beauvais-Tillé** (BVA), which lies in Tillé near Beauvais, about 80km outside

BIARRITZ TRAVEL GUIDE

Paris, is primarily used by Ryanair for its flights connecting Paris to Dublin, Shannon Glasgow and other cities.

There are several important regional airports. **Aéroport Nice Côte d'Azur** (NCE) is the 3rd busiest airport in France and serves as a gateway to the popular French Riviera. **Aéroport Lyon Saint-Exupéry** (LYS) lies 20km east of Lyon and serves as the main hub for connections to the French Alps and Provence. It is the 4th busiest airport of France. **Aéroport de Bordeaux** (BOD) served the region of Bordeaux. **Aéroport de Toulouse – Blagnac** (TLS), which lies 7km from Toulouse, provides access to the south-western part of France. **Aéroport de Strasbourg** (SXB), which lies 10km west of Strasbourg, served as a connection to Orly, Paris and Nice. **Aéroport de Marseille Provence** (MRS) is located in the town of Marignane, about 27km from Marseille and provides access to Provence and the French Riviera. **Aéroport Nantes Atlantique** (NTE) lies in Bouguenais, 8km from Nantes carriers and provides a gateway to the regions of Normandy and Brittany in the western part of France. **Aéroport de Lille** (LIL) is located near Lesquin and provides connections to the northern part of France.

🌐 Airlines

Air France is the national flag carrier of France and in 2003, it merged with KLM. The airline has a Flying Blue rewards

BIARRITZ TRAVEL GUIDE

program, which allows members to earn, accumulate and redeem Flying Blue Miles on any flights with Air France, KLM or any other Sky Team airline. This includes Aeroflot, Aerolineas Argentinas, AeroMexico, Air Europa, Alitalia, China Airlines, China Eastern, China Southern, Czech Airlines, Delta, Garuda Indonesia, Kenya Airways, Korean Air, Middle Eastern Airlines, Saudia, Tarom, Vietnam Airlines and Xiamen Airlines.

Air France operates several subsidiaries, including the low-cost Transavia.com France, Cityjet and Hop! It is also in partnership with Air Corsica. Other French airlines are Corsairfly and XL Airways France (formerly Star Airlines).

France's largest intercontinental airport, Charles de Gaulle serves as a hub for Air France, as well as its regional subsidiary, HOP!. It also functions as a European hub for Delta Airlines. Orly Airport, also in Paris, serves as the main hub for Air France's low cost subsidiary, Transavia, with 40 different destinations, including London, Madrid, Copenhagen, Moscow, Casablanca, Algiers, Amsterdam, Istanbul, Venice, Rome, Berlin and Athens. Aéroport de Marseille Provence (MRS) outside Marseille serves as a hub to the region for budget airlines such as EasyJet and Ryanair. Aéroport Nantes Atlantique serves as a French base for the Spanish budget airline, Volotea.

BIARRITZ TRAVEL GUIDE

🌐 Currency

France's currency is the Euro. It is issued in notes in denominations of €500, €200, €100, €50, €20, €10 and €5. Coins are issued in €2, €1, 50c, 20c, 10c, 5c, 2c and 1c.

🌐 Banking & ATMs

If your ATM card is compatible with the MasterCard/Cirrus or Visa/Plus networks and configured for a 4-digit PIN, you will have no problem drawing money in France. Most French ATMs have an English language option. Remember to inform your bank of your travel plans before you leave. Keep an eye open around French ATMs to avoid pickpockets or scammers.

🌐 Credit Cards

Credit cards are frequently used throughout France, not just in shops, but also to pay for metro tickets, parking tickets, and motorway tolls and even to make phone calls at phone booths. MasterCard and Visa are accepted by most vendors. American Express and Diners Club are also accepted by the more tourist oriented businesses. Credit cards issued in Europe are smart cards that that are fitted with a microchip and require a PIN for each transaction. This means that a few ticket machines, self-service vendors and other businesses may not be configured to accept the older magnetic strip credit cards.

🌐 Tourist Taxes

All visitors to France pay a compulsory city tax or tourist tax ("taxe de séjour"), which is payable at your accommodation. Children are exempt from tourist tax. The rate depends on the standard of accommodation, starting with €0.75 per night for cheaper establishments going up to €4, for the priciest options. Rates are, of course, subject to change.

🌐 Reclaiming VAT

If you are not from the European Union, you can claim back VAT (or Value Added Tax) paid on your purchases in France. The VAT rate in France is 20 percent on most goods, but restaurant goods, food, transport and medicine are charged at lower rates. VAT can be claimed back on purchases of over €175 from the same shop, provided that your stay in France does not exceed six months. Look for shops that display a "Tax Free" sign. The shop assistant must fill out a form for reclaiming VAT. When you submit it at the airport, you can expect your refund to be debited within 30 to 90 days to your credit card or bank account. It can also be sent by cheque.

🌐 Tipping Policy

In French restaurants, a 15 percent service charge is added directly to your bill and itemized with the words *service compris* or "tip included". This is a legal requirement for taxation purposes. If the service was unusually good, a little extra will be appreciated. In an expensive restaurant where there is a coat check, you may add €1 per coat. In a few other situations, a tip will be appreciated. You can give an usherette in a theatre 50 cents to €1, give a porter €1 per bag for helping with your luggage or show your appreciation for a taxi driver with 5-10 percent over the fare. It is also customary to tip a hair dresser or a tour guide 10 percent.

🌐 Mobile Phones

Most EU countries, including France uses the GSM mobile service. This means that most UK phones and some US and Canadian phones and mobile devices will work in France. While you could check with your service provider about coverage before you leave, using your own service in roaming mode will involve additional costs. The alternative is to purchase a French SIM card to use during your stay in France. France has four mobile networks. They are Orange, SFR, Bouygues Telecom and Free. In France, foreigners are barred from applying for regular phone contract and the data rates are somewhat pricier on pre-paid phone services than in most European countries. You will need to show some form of identification, such as a passport when you make your purchase and it can take up to 48 hours to activate a French SIM card. If there is an Orange Boutique nearby, you can buy a SIM for €3.90. Otherwise, the Orange Holiday package is available for €39.99. Orange also sells a 4G device which enables your own portable Wi-Fi hotspot for €54.90. SFR offers a SIM card, simply known as le card for €9.99. Data rates begin at €5 for 20Mb.

Dialling Code

The international dialling code for France is +33.

Emergency Numbers

All emergencies: (by mobile) 112
Police: 17
Medical Assistance: 15
Fire and Accidents: 18
SOS All Emergencies (hearing assisted: 114)
Visa: 0800 90 11 79
MasterCard: 0800 90 13 87
American Express: 0800 83 28 20

Public Holidays

1 January: New Year's Day (Nouvel an / Jour de l'an / Premier de l'an)

BIARRITZ TRAVEL GUIDE

March - April: Easter Monday (Lundi de Pâques)

1 May: Labor Day (Fête du Travail / Fête des Travailleurs)

8 May: Victory in Europe Day (Fête de la Victoire)

May: Ascension Day (Ascension)

May: Whit Monday (Lundi de Pentecôte)

14 July: Bastille Day (Fête nationale)

15 August: Assumption of Mary (L'Assomption de Marie)

1 November: All Saints Day (La Toussaint)

11 November: Armistace Day (Armistice de 1918)

25 December: Christmas Day (Noël)

Good Friday and St Stephens Day (26 December) are observed only in Alsace and Moselle.

Time Zone

France falls in the Central European Time Zone. This can be calculated as Greenwich Mean Time/Co-ordinated Universal Time (GMT/UTC) +2; Eastern Standard Time (North America) -6; Pacific Standard Time (North America) -9.

Daylight Savings Time

Clocks are set forward one hour on the last Sunday of March and set back one hour on the last Sunday of October for Daylight Savings Time.

BIARRITZ TRAVEL GUIDE

🌐 School Holidays

The academic year in France is from the beginning of September to the end of June. The long summer holiday is from the beginning of July to the end of August. There are three shorter vacation periods. All schools break up for a two week break around Christmas and New Year. There are also two week breaks in February and April, but this varies per region, as French schools are divided into three zones, which take their winter and spring vacations at different times.

🌐 Driving Laws

The French drive on the ride hand side of the road. If you have a non-European driving licence, you will be able to use it in France, provided that the licence is valid and was issued in your country of residence before the date of your visa application. There are a few other provisions. The minimum driving age in France is 18. Your licence will need to be in French or alternately, you must carry a French translation of your driving permit with you.

In France, the speed limit depends on weather conditions. In dry weather, the speed limit is 130km per hour for highways, 110km per hour for 4-lane expressways and 90km per hour for 2 or 3-lane rural roads. In rainy weather, this is reduced to 110km, 100km and 80km per hour respectively. In foggy weather with poor visibility, the speed limit is 50km per hour on all roads. On urban roads, the speed limit is also 50km per hour.

By law, French drivers are obliged to carry a breathalyser in their vehicle, but these are available from most supermarkets, chemists and garages for €1. The legal limit is 0.05, but for new drivers who have had their licence for less than three years, it is 0.02. French motorways are called autorouts. It is illegal in France to use a mobile phone while driving, even if you have a headset.

🌍 Drinking Laws

The legal drinking age in France is 18. The drinking policy regarding public spaces will seem confusing to outsiders. Each municipal area imposes its own laws. In Paris, alcohol consumption is only permitted in licensed establishments. It is strictly forbidden in parks and public gardens.

🌍 Smoking Laws

From 2007, smoking has been banned in indoor spaces such as schools, government buildings, airports, offices and factories in France. The ban was extended in 2008 to hospitality venues such as restaurants, bars, cafes and casinos. French trains have been smoke free since December 2004.

BIARRITZ TRAVEL GUIDE

🌐 Electricity

Electricity: 220-240 volts

Frequency: 50 Hz

Electricity sockets in France are unlike those of any other country. They are hermaphroditic, meaning that they come equipped with both prongs and indents. When visiting from the UK, Ireland, the USA or even another European country, you will need a special type of adaptor to accommodate this. If travelling from the USA, you will also need a converter or step-down transformer to convert the current to to 110 volts, to avoid damage to your appliances. The latest models of many laptops, camcorders, mobile phones and digital cameras are dual-voltage with a built in converter.

🌐 Food & Drink

France is a paradise for dedicated food lovers and the country has a vast variety of well-known signature dishes. These include foie gras, bouillabaisse, escargots de Bourgogne, Coq au vin, Bœuf Bourguignon, quiche Lorraine and ratatouille. A great budget option is crêpes or pancakes. Favorite sweets and pastries include éclairs, macarons, mille-feuilles, crème brûlée and croissants.

The country is home to several world-famous wine-growing regions, including Alsace, Bordeaux, Bourgogne, Champagne,

Corse, Côtes du Rhône, Languedoc-Roussillon, Loire, Provence and Sud-Ouest and correctly matching food to complimentary wine choices is practically a science. Therein lies the key to enjoying wine as the French do. It accompanies the meal. Drinking wine when it is not lunch or dinner time is sure to mark you as a foreigner. Pastis and dry vermouth are popular aperitifs and favorite after-dinner digestifs include cognac, Armagnac, calvados and eaux de vie. The most popular French beer is Kronenbourg, which originates from a brewery that dates back to 1664.

Websites

http://www.rendezvousenfrance.com/

http://www.france.com/

http://www.francethisway.com/

http://www.france-voyage.com/en/

http://www.francewanderer.com/

http://wikitravel.org/en/France

http://www.bonjourlafrance.com/index.aspx

Printed in Great Britain
by Amazon